ESSENTIAL SPELLING LIST

3,200 EVERYDAY WORDS

CAREFULLY SELECTED AND GRADED INTO SIX LISTS
SUITABLE FOR CHILDREN OF AGES 7-12. WORDS
WITHIN EACH LIST ARE GROUPED ACCORDING
TO COMMON DIFFICULTY TO FACILITATE
LEARNING

FRED J. SCHONELL, M.A., Ph.D., D.Lit.

PROFESSOR OF EDUCATION, UNIVERSITY OF QUEENSLAND
FORMERLY PROFESSOR OF EDUCATION, UNIVERSITY OF BIRMINGHAM

M
MACMILLAN EDUCATION

FOREWORD

" THE ESSENTIAL SPELLING LIST " is a body of words which Elementary School Children most commonly use in writing. The words have been distributed into six Groups on the principle that a child should be taught a word when he wants to write it. Hence the Groups, suitable for children aged 7-12, are definitely of increasing difficulty, while the words within each Group become, in the main, successively harder.

It is intended that the words should constitute the basic material for curricula requirements in the Elementary School. If a child has mastered these he can spell most of the words he wishes to write and 80-90 per cent of those found in the majority of books and newspapers. It is intended too that each Group should provide words sufficient for the spelling lessons of a school year. Although the basis of both selection and grading has been frequency of child usage, yet in all cases the lists should be sparingly supplemented with words of local significance, composition requirements and specific experiences. It is not intended that a particular Group should be used with a particular class, or that it is only suitable to children of a particular age. Use of a Group will vary considerably with the intellectual calibre of the class. Selection of Group will best be determined by the discerning class teacher himself, but results indicate that the following assignments are most suitable:

FOREWORD

				No. of Words	Age
Group 1	-	-	-	396	7
Group 2	-	-	-	456	8
Group 3	-	-	-	544	9
Group 4	-	-	-	576	10
Group 5	-	-	-	600	11
Group 6	-	-	-	600	12

The words have been arranged in small units of a day's assignment, varying from three in the first to five in the final list. Furthermore, in most instances the fourth unit contains words similar in structure to those studied on the three previous days. The reproduction of a specimen set from Group 3 better exemplifies the underlying principles of construction.

team	slave	front
steam	shave	month
scream	grave	Monday
gleam	cape	ton

shape	treat	won	wonder

It will be noticed that there are only four units in a set, as it was thought that the fifth day might profitably be spent in reviewing all words of the preceding four days' assignments.

To meet the need for periodic revision sixty Graded Dictation Reviews,[1] ten for each Group, have been carefully compiled. The Graded Reviews provide practice in writing prose from dictation and eliminate the injurious effects that sometimes accrue from repeated use of difficult unseen passages.

[1] Included in *Essentials in Teaching and Testing Spelling.*

F. J. SCHONELL.

ACKNOWLEDGMENTS

THE Author gratefully acknowledges his indebtedness to many teachers and children who, by taking part in classroom trial with the words, helped considerably in the preparation of the List, and particularly to his wife who spent long hours assisting in the selection, grading and grouping of the words. In addition he owes a debt to Professor Horn's publication, *A Basic Writing Vocabulary—10,000 Words Most Commonly used in Writing*, which resulted from a careful analysis of written material involving 5,136,000 words.

CONTENTS

PAGE

GROUP 1—396 EVERYDAY WORDS SUITABLE FOR
CHILDREN AGE 7   6

GROUP 2—456 EVERYDAY WORDS SUITABLE FOR
CHILDREN AGE 8   12

GROUP 3—544 EVERYDAY WORDS SUITABLE FOR
CHILDREN AGE 9   19

GROUP 4—576 EVERYDAY WORDS SUITABLE FOR
CHILDREN AGE 10   26

GROUP 5—600 EVERYDAY WORDS SUITABLE FOR
CHILDREN AGE 11   33

GROUP 6—600 EVERYDAY WORDS SUITABLE FOR
CHILDREN AGE 12   41

GROUP 1

man	get	run
can	wet	gun
ran	let	sun

met fun ant

red	did	hot
bed	hid	not
fed	lid	blot

spot led lip

had	bud	tell
sad	mud	fell
glad	rug	bell

dug well has

pin	pet	top
tin	set	stop
win	leg	shop

peg dog tip

ill	bat	nut
hill	that	cut
will	bag	but

rag fill shut

rub	sit		yes
tub	bit		yet
dust	dig		pen
	open fog	pig	

look	kill		cap
book	till		tap
took	mill		clap
	cook trap	still	

all	men		here
ball	ten		where
fall	then		there
	small egg	when	

end	sing		good
send	king		wood
mend	thing		foot
	boot lend	them	

ring	old		call
bring	hold		tall
spring	told		wall
	gold bold	calling	

him	was		her
his	wash		she
this	want		they
	sum drum	what	

see	six	by
tree	fix	cry
been	box	try

sky   sweet   fox

name	our	wish
came	out	dish
game	about	fish

same   you   your

ink	eat	take
drink	sea	cake
milk	read	make

rich   much   made

God	far	put
soft	car	pull
from	cart	full

doll   clean   part

hand	jam	long
sand	jar	song
land	jump	for

are   morning   stand

nest	ship	say
best	slip	day
rest	skip	to-day

saw   help   play

SPELLING LIST

age	ride	deep
cage	side	keep
page	hide	sleep

time feet into

bite	may	ever
white	way	every
like	away	never

stay mile very

coat	went	ice
boat	sent	nice
road	bent	drop

with sell bend

head	mine	room
bread	line	moon
lost	nine	soon

school have five

pay	rope	cup
bay	hope	pup
hay	hole	under

pole lay said

pipe	feed	now
wipe	need	cow
ripe	sheep	how

were paper down

A 2

boy	gave	round
toy	give	ground
flag	live	found

count   hall   mouth

rain	find	home
train	kind	nose
again	wind	rose

going   doing   raining

other	father	ate
mother	winter	late
brother	summer	gate

sister   able   table

dinner	back	fly
supper	black	dry
butter	sick	seven

water   bill   duck

snow	kitten	sorry
blow	letter	funny
grow	lesson	sunny

little   show   happy

arm	girl	one
hard	bird	love
dark	first	come

coming   making   river

spoke	hair	pretty
smoke	chair	dress
fire	fair	grass

baby   story   fairy

fast	sold	penny
last	cold	add
each	colder	apple

over   only   after

ear	talk	house
hear	walk	mouse
dear	horse	than

year   near   ask

face	eye	more
race	eyes	store
left	tail	plant

wait   miss   lady

GROUP 2

lamp	rent	wing
camp	spent	swing
damp	spend	sting

stamp   string   west

spin	rock	lump
skin	lock	pump
plan	clock	blunt

block   stick   plum

seed	hang	pick
weed	sang	brick
bleed	rang	trick

seem   pack   crack

pond	rush	band
fond	brush	bank
chop	crush	thank

just   shot   chin

cave	shell	dive
wave	smell	drive
save	swell	driver

brave   crane   safe

hood	club	lake
stood	hunt	bake
hook	hunter	baker

rise   sake   spoon

meet	rake	lift
street	wake	list
sheet	awake	mist

week   three   named

date	bee	fine
hate	free	shine
plate	queen	pine

mate   case   chase

creep	chain	pile
sleep	pain	smile
asleep	paint	while

sleeping   painting   waiting

cost	wide	lace
frost	slide	place
frog	life	grand

wife   son   grandfather

push	myself	moth
bush	herself	hoped
stem	himself	kiss

itself   neck   body

fold	mind	snap
scold	wild	strap
held	child	both

blind   children   another

lick	horn	crab
kick	born	swim
thick	gas	storm

quick   joy   ticket

park	tea	most
bark	teach	post
mark	teacher	stamp

market   corn   corner

poor	roof	yard
door	window	card
floor	broom	garden

bedroom   shade   spade

barn	less	meat
harm	bless	heat
farm	press	beat

neat   such   farmer

fear	pass	town
clear	class	brown
heard	glass	flower

belt   leaf   bunch

pink	east	sail
think	feast	pail
flat	beast	nail

fail   mix   least

lame	drill	cream
blame	spill	dream
tame	spell	meal

spelling   shame   suck

die	pool	turn
pie	cool	burn
lie	food	hurt

lies   church   curl

oak	ready	sir
goat	dead	dirt
load	death	firm

shirt   third   died

air	night	word
pair	right	world
stair	bright	forget

upstairs   downstairs   to-night

inside	low	star
outside	slow	start
within	crow	sharp

without   own   throw

bow	walking	walked
row	talking	talked
follow	thinking	asked

looked   looking   maid

who	nor	speak
which	doctor	speaking
why	fork	reading

pork   trip   whip

opening	alive	loud
opened	along	cloud
washed	became	hour

north   south   filled

playground	master	babies
football	basket	ladies
march	tiny	stories

new   party   dance

having	tooth	seen
giving	teeth	green
living	bath	feel

riding   heel   once

cherry	jelly	carry
cherries	jolly	carried
berries	to-morrow	shall

berry   merry   marry

rice	paw	bean
mice	raw	lean
pence	draw	mean

lead   beads   gay

crying	flies	beach
cried	cries	reach
tried	tries	easy

warm   please   great

skipping	stopped	bigger
dropping	dropped	biggest
running	getting	better

their   two   slippers

before	any	fresh
below	many	felt
belong	anything	melt

nothing   beside   behind

oil	few	know
boil	dew	knew
join	drew	grew

blew   off   point

pound	kept	use
sound	desk	used
bound	key	puppy

even   ox   oxen

sale	learn	would
tale	early	could
later	strong	cross

these those thin

number	note	played
ruler	woke	stayed
uncle	stone	clever

drove whole next

done	does	true
gone	goes	blue
bone	inch	silk

some longer longest

GROUP 3

team	slave	front
steam	shave	month
scream	grave	Monday
gleam	cape	ton

shape   treat   won   wonder

paying	upper	rode
playing	sudden	globe
saying	suffer	joke
staying	offer	poker

pray   plays   flutter   close

vain	thunder	soil
plain	peal	spoil
obtain	stuck	noise
faint	struck	swift

shock   burst   moment   rainbow

pocket	needle	light
silver	button	sight
money	sew	might
honey	print	fight

stockings   high   sigh   fright

robber	real	proud
ladder	deal	pride
bottom	steal	spite
rabbit	leap	rage

bear   wear   tear   pear

singing	begin	prince
bringing	began	princess
blowing	begun	crown
feeling	music	crowd

lord   state   gain   main

sow	turnip	vine
grain	straw	wine
wheat	claw	grape
pea	drawing	field

depart   travel   return   remain

animal	port	prison
donkey	tide	pardon
monkey	shore	forgive
monkeys	coast	punish

lion   rude   swan   polite

gather	owl	arrow
rather	growl	narrow
path	chicken	sorrow
enter	crust	borrow

yellow   pillow   understand   understood

shallow	anger	pale
stream	hunger	shake
moss	hungry	snake
carpet	drank	danger

wade   trade   sash   splash

March	form	large
April	thorn	charge
May	marble	strange
trust	tumble	stranger

someone   something   sometimes   stable

sort	Sunday	dusty
sport	Thursday	stormy
handle	Friday	frosty
candle	unless	cloudy

anybody   nobody   happen   cannot

lamb	sleepy	stove
comb	dirty	glove
crumb	busy	cover
thumb	lucky	shelter

climb   steady   none   become

brain	power	roll
brow	shower	rolled
chest	tower	rolling
cheek	towel	pulled

heart   act   cottage   pudding

match	June	picking
catch	July	picked
patch	September	learned
watch	November	reached

fetch   ditch   snatch   everyone

care	infant	tender
careless	darling	gentle
useless	cradle	weak
useful	young	dull

purse   nurse   fur   beak

hammer	too	lunch
bench	tool	buy
blade	stool	beef
wire	fool	cloth

blood   goose   geese   cheese

change	break	brighter
changed	broke	brightest
taken	broken	safer
eaten	stole	safest

cooler   deeper   finer   miner

hiding	skate	chief
shining	skating	thief
smiling	darkness	grief
hoping	illness	burnt

should   cheer   quickly   nearly

write	prove	gray
writing	move	clay
wrote	remove	poem
wrap	repeat	poet

remark   repair   Easter   Christmas

aloud	coal	yesterday
around	roast	afternoon
alike	cloak	however
afraid	float	breakfast

roam   grandmother   above   usual

branch	classes	together
branches	glasses	towards
peach	order	afterwards
peaches	border	forward

inches   worth   starve   husband

price	pepper	visit
twice	copper	fir
since	cuff	birth
fence	stuff	birthday

bitter   silly   stiff   hurry

provide	dwell	friend
pretend	present	quiet
forest	lemon	boxes
track	sugar	dishes

finger   flesh   wool   bloom

cling	serve	four
strip	person	fourth
pint	term	fifth
gift	upset	tenth

eleven   simple   twelve   hundred

daisy	wise	earn
daisies	spider	earth
lily	soap	grace
lilies	soak	space

voice   bravely   invite   chance

steep	thirteen	thirty
steel	fourteen	twenty
wheel	fifteen	fifty
deed	sixteen	sixty

thousand   creeping   indeed   between

half	halves	flew
calf	leaves	threw
shelf	thieves	crew
loaf	loaves	chew

wolf   themselves   grind   thrown

knee	knife	mail
kneel	knives	rail
knot	wives	snail
knock	fixed	jail

flock   finish   tie   tied

raise	cure	capture
raised	sure	defend
trunk	pure	dying
strike	picture	lying

dread   deaf   heaven   paid

built	battle	kettle
build	rattle	bottle
building	cattle	cork
content	tired	sore

rate   flame   frame   scrape

swimming	toe	trying
slipped	scout	flying
matter	shout	army
manner	axe	rank

shy   spy   butterfly   answer

heavy	easier	cause
heavier	easiest	because
heaviest	easily	instant
war	merrily	shadow

arch   starch   touch   being

past	copy	taste
mast	pity	waste
fasten	empty	haste
odd	plenty	good-bye

loss   lose   glory   history

GROUP 4

manage	remind	slice
savage	respond	spice
package	repent	notice
postage	record	police

report import export forty

proper	damage	silent
property	voyage	parent
consist	advantage	absent
conduct	wages	serpent

prevent silence remarkable blanket

purple	former	also
furnish	organ	almost
curtain	orchard	already
Saturday	coward	always

murder altogether although comfort

harvest	perhaps	pitch
garment	permit	stitch
alarm	perfect	kitchen
farther	sermon	stretch

cargo artist enjoy enjoyed

tease	oven	linen
weave	woven	often
preach	golden	hasten
beneath	dozen	listen

cheap   seam   eagle   eager

hotel	armour	intend
camel	parlour	inspect
label	colour	interest
angel	favour	kingdom

favourite   bacon   apron   grasp

castle	grown	fare
thistle	blown	bare
whistle	widow	dare
whisper	velvet	stare

human   woman   women   spare

stain	explain	idle
contain	expect	island
captain	express	share
Britain	extent	pantry

fountain   mountain   certain   extra

paddle	playmate	hoof
meddle	newspaper	smooth
middle	platform	stoop
cripple	fortnight	stooped

settle   midday   midnight   choose

draper	county	limit
grate	country	spirit
scale	cousin	timid
escape	message	public

Wales   Scotland   England   English

laugh	lately	motor
laughed	safely	visitor
laughter	nicely	victory
linger	lovely	inform

lonely   likely   likeness   weakness

servant	though	arrive
merchant	through	advice
distant	empire	adventure
important	admire	nature

constant   admit   amuse   ashamed

evening	object	sailor
event	subject	tailor
equator	robin	railway
enough	holiday	daily

rough   tough   rainy   rocky

sparrow	village	ought
swallow	cabbage	bought
valley	carrot	brought
valleys	gallop	fought

thought   ragged   scatter   brass

alone	nasty	vanish
across	hasty	banish
among	shady	perish
against	study	parish

fancy   ugly   polish   Welsh

lawn	lays	beauty
dawn	laying	beautiful
famous	laid	careful
dangerous	thankful	carefully

faithfully   welcome   until   unable

glance	protect	stumble
advance	monster	grumble
distance	bough	thimble
France	plough	tremble

scramble   bundle   kindle   noble

tight	bucket	error
slight	trumpet	terror
delight	shrub	ribbon
mighty	liberty	cotton

Scottish   mutton   blossom   correct

chalk	gaze	discover
stalk	blaze	distinct
salt	razor	discuss
alter	lazy	distress

size   prize   dislike   disgrace

nation	company	rubber
station	companion	bullet
dictation	astonish	quarrel
motion	publish	barrel

question   appear   quart   quarter

horrid	belief	wharf
coffee	believe	wharves
occur	grieve	niece
occurred	ourselves	piece

occupy   hollow   forgotten   combine

caught	stir	knit
taught	stirred	knitting
daughter	mirror	knight
naughty	bonnet	skill

office   officer   different   skirt

potato	value	instead
potatoes	continue	steadily
tomato	statue	weary
tomatoes	thread	wearily

foe   poetry   butcher   shilling

tunnel	pleasant	groan
suppose	pleasure	coach
cunning	measure	toast
muddy	treasure	throat

defeat   tiger   reward   shoe

obey	dwelling	group
obeyed	wedding	wound
swept	herring	youth
crept	vessel	calm

prettier   prettiest   beginning   journey

recall	demand	feather
result	deliver	leather
beyond	depend	weather
shiver	delay	breath

health   healthy   wealthy   meant

fleet	drown	aim
screen	drowned	claim
greedy	powder	praise
freedom	petrol	dairy

deer   steer   queer   engage

guilty	season	medal
guide	reason	metal
guest	crimson	mental
warn	iron	board

Briton   British   Irish   Ireland

relate	desire	bathe
retire	deserve	vase
restore	behave	rare
refuse	bravery	square

December   October   Germany   herd

attend	edge	flour
attack	hedge	sour
wreck	badge	trout
wrong	judge	stout

lodge   bridge   sword   check

suit	member	wore
fruit	remember	score
orange	remembered	whom
banana	memory	whether

bowl   factory   basement   pavement

using	eight	figure
during	weight	scripture
duty	weigh	creature
truth	dumb	entertain

pour   court   shoulder   huge

exchange	reply	worship
except	drying	worse
excuse	carrying	worst
piano	foggy	worry

city   cities   circle   palace

giant	coin	earnest
engine	noisy	search
divide	sign	French
mistake	signal	honest

seldom   quite   wicked   selfish

throne	area		local
choke	idea		several
clothes	family		second
owe	people		fortune
cruel	Tuesday	Wednesday	disgust

picnic	aunt	pencil
arithmetic	saucer	ocean
flood	farewell	collar
wooden	else	clumsy

holy pony navy losing

GROUP 5

address	regret		lawyer
afford	regard		gardener
assist	retreat		passenger
approach	respect		drawer
account	nerve		chapter
apply allow	allowed	clown	refer

direct	ankle	confess
detect	sparkle	confine
destroy	humble	confuse
destroyed	feeble	consider
describe	steeple	convict

vote devote vast plaster pastime

inhabit	educate	pupil
insist	education	peril
invent	information	profit
industry	position	credit
increase	composition	splendid

stupid   insect   sole   dose   whose

future	dismiss	final
pasture	display	finally
furniture	dismay	gradual
manufacture	disorder	gradually
departure	disappear	usually

failure   total   equal   equally   really

Africa	breeze	wonderful
America	freeze	respectful
Canada	squeeze	awful
Atlantic	sleeve	yawn
Pacific	agreeable	fully

China   Arctic   frozen   degree   gem

hero	pickle	climate
heroes	knuckle	private
negro	trample	cultivate
negroes	title	decorate
echo	entitle	decoration

chorus   single   jungle   article   measles

Europe	mere	fraction
Asia	merely	direction
India	sincere	condition
Australia	sincerely	reduction
Russia	severe	protection

telephone   switch   sketch   lantern   fern

terrible	saddle	northern
horrible	struggle	southern
possible	puzzle	eastern
impossible	latter	western
improve	parrot	shepherd

limb   modern   modest   screw   nephew

double	dispute	regular
trouble	displease	popular
couple	disobey	particular
courage	district	singular
encourage	disturb	vinegar

flourish   prey   victim   cigar   calendar

erect	canal	mistress
elect	capital	misfortune
election	rural	mischief
electric	mortal	handkerchief
halt	funeral	handsome

trial   loyal   royal   rascal   musical

detain	procure	revive
retain	endure	revenge
complain	feature	reverse
bargain	torture	resolve
waist	secure	resemble

secret   select   request   require   inquire

ordinary	image	exact
library	imagine	exactly
January	imagination	expand
February	examine	extract
enemy	examination	exercise

exist   example   bury   buried   ivy

loan	preserve	fortunate
coax	prepare	unfortunate
oath	compare	moderate
active	beware	estimate
action	betray	happiness

compose   advise   promise   glimpse   sense

wrestle	beggar	produce
wrist	cellar	promote
written	pillar	progress
gentlemen	grammar	possess
heathen	burglar	entire

chimney   turkey   tune   tube   costume

discontent	grocer	mention
represent	groceries	attention
evident	tempt	situation
frequent	attempt	invitation
accident	temptation	truly

elbow   growth   speech   graze   naked

accept	honour	labour
according	harbour	devour
plunge	habit	justice
population	pigeon	practice
satin	gulf	service

sober   basin   cabin   rapid   payment

excite	construct	explore
exciting	contribute	exploration
excellent	consume	explanation
exclaim	confirm	style
exclaimed	contrast	pavement

expel   angry   envy   idea   oblige

height	junior	gospel
either	language	compel
neither	monument	chapel
reign	department	jewel
foreign	swear	bushel

parcel   course   veil   vein   neighbour

supply	avenue	government
support	diamond	madam
attract	foundation	passage
arrest	fuel	bandage
shrink	cruelly	separate

enclose   entry   magic   dye   ruin

latitude	employ	observe
altitude	employer	observation
minute	custom	desert
reduce	customer	slavery
refuge	fever	misery

violin   violet   cricket   clerk   onion

common	errand	arrange
collect	funnel	arranging
connect	flannel	gallery
connection	channel	difficult
command	current	umbrella

neglect   cruiser   suspect   villain   cannon

argue	citizen	surprise
argument	century	purchase
valuable	centre	purpose
vegetable	central	further
comfortable	hospital	scratch

complete   estate   minister   receive   deceive

scare	insane	entrance
scarce	invade	performance
scarf	inspire	balance
meanness	include	substance
straight	introduce	lightning

dodge   pledge   divine   ache   headache

adopt	guard	decide
prompt	guess	recite
cupboard	guinea	concert
sponge	tongue	fertile
problem	rogue	unite

mercy   multiply   ninth   fashion   thirsty

uniform	expense	ninety
perform	expensive	safety
force	relative	surely
skull	standard	entirely
utmost	scholar	o'clock

period   roar   soar   cocoa   situated

general	embrace	threat
generally	surface	weapon
practical	furnace	forehead
natural	wasp	heaviness
naturally	sleepiness	weariness

annual   cough   ounce   soup   business

bicycle	permission	orphan
biscuit	admission	geography
juice	million	elephant
statement	region	abundant
improvement	union	colony

sentence defence peace appeal instantly

author	August	brief
governor	autumn	priest
conductor	fault	shriek
scent	pause	fierce
scene	laundry	view

scenery length depth submit subtract

choice	curious	arouse
rejoice	various	trousers
avoid	glorious	surround
moisture	anxious	surrender
palm	worthy	wither

abrupt lungs fury material special

woollen	carriage	succeed
crooked	marriage	success
loose	machine	successful
foolish	acre	prayer
soldier	pearl	deny

New Zealand zone debt doubt

GROUP 6

personal	declare	portion
liberal	decrease	proportion
festival	decline	production
removal	determine	protection
criminal	determination	introduction

fund minor major majority traitor

greet	accurate	insult
Greece	accuse	instruct
engineer	accustom	insert
pioneer	announce	injure
career	addition	injury

keen ghost skeleton cushion income

contract	prefer	wholesome
control	preferred	enterprise
consent	conferred	therefore
contempt	grudge	wireless
conclude	lodging	grateful

convince poison coil wisdom condemn

hesitate	continent	stage
delicate	fragment	garage
candidate	regiment	average
certificate	experiment	discourage
navigate	cement	baggage

debate student confident camera remedy

treaty	lecture	nervous
treatment	agriculture	prosperous
ornament	temperate	tremendous
instrument	temperature	ridiculous
prominent	puncture	jealous

recent recently volcano couch route

sensible	ignorant	ceiling
responsible	ignorance	perceive
visible	abundance	deceit
invisible	attendance	deceitful
rifle	appearance	earthquake

hatred sacred witch wretched wrinkle

telescope	national	conversation
telegram	cathedral	consideration
telegraph	principal	sensation
photograph	punctual	combination
physical	continually	ventilation

phrase fatal section intention choir

domestic	tenant	fragrant
athletic	vacant	insurance
heroic	tyrant	assistance
majestic	elegant	remembrance
tropics	extravagant	circumstance

item ideal pilot pistol seize

miserable	despair	convert
reasonable	despise	concern
capable	description	convey
probable	destruction	witness
probably	energy	cleanliness

liable　reliable　angle　trifle　muscle

influence	famine	reception
presence	medicine	ambition
evidence	genuine	satisfaction
residence	granite	objection
reference	definite	instruction

absence　pretence　umpire　crime　circus

salute	detail	acquire
distribute	deposit	acquaint
gratitude	develop	acquainted
destitute	strength	acquaintance
volume	strengthen	disappoint

luxury　burden　swollen　execute　abbey

pattern	release	offend
messenger	reveal	oppose
traveller	reflect	opposite
challenge	reserve	opposition
college	remainder	application

response　resign　design　oppress　approve

flavour
vapour
rumour
occasion
occasionally

generous
numerous
enormous
mischievous
marvellous

innocent
independent
excitement
advertise
advertisement

practise impudent yield shield pierce

invalid
invention
patient
impatient
impatience

digest
digestion
soul
mould
poultry

provoke
proclaim
pronounce
proceed
opinion

frigid civil civilized operation heir

commit
commence
recommend
recollect
shipping

comrade
complaint
humour
endeavour
tobacco

pension
provision
decision
conclusion
division

solve dissolve wholly annoy annoyed

poverty
mutiny
variety
society
sacrifice

margin
origin
original
moral
crystal

transform
translate
character
programme
sandwich

arrival Spain dainty quaint quench

create	suitable	Chinese
creation	creditable	interfere
emigrate	honourable	supreme
emigrant	peaceable	extreme
obstinate	manageable	extremely

scheme   pursue   pursuit   mourn   source

intelligent	judgment	thorough
intelligence	parliament	sustain
difference	incident	maintain
offence	magnificent	portrait
apparent	compliment	quarry

torrent   squirrel   essay   type   typewriter

vulgar	boundary	convenient
similar	tributary	convenience
irregular	missionary	experience
circular	salary	obedient
military	extraordinary	obedience

existence   consequence   psalm   attach   fowl

ascend	plague	obstacle
descend	league	miracle
science	fatigue	spectacle
scissors	disguise	violent
intimate	disaster	permanent

rear   breathe   cease   conceal   awkward

university	social	precious
opportunity	artificial	gracious
possibility	especially	delicious
responsibility	musician	suspicious
curiosity	triumph	suspicion

charity   ability   brooch   stomach   wreath

religion	necessary	exceed
religious	necessity	exclude
previous	furious	exception
victorious	serious	expedition
industrious	behaviour	explode

solemn   prophet   scarlet   excursion   saviour

distinguish	system	persevere
extinguish	sympathy	atmosphere
persuade	mystery	electricity
establish	delivery	interrupt
diminish	discovery	settler

abolish   leisure   sovereign   urge   urgent

pressure	affection	scribble
assure	affectionate	ruffle
assume	attraction	rubbish
assent	accomplish	summit
assemble	accompany	traffic

appoint   affair   twilight   coarse   hoarse

nursery	organize	occupation
jewellery	organization	congregation
machinery	realize	preparation
prospect	recognize	separation
satisfy	horizon	champion

collection   attractive   novel   marvel   cancel

celebrate	passion	interior
celebration	impression	exterior
illustrate	discussion	inferior
chocolate	possession	superior
immediately	correspond	senior

imitate   imitation   soothe   indulge   indulging

benefit	audience	exhaust
benefited	authority	exhibit
profited	clause	exhibition
partner	applaud	register
privilege	cautious	nourish

launch   breadth   suburb   council   album

nonsense	knowledge	instructor
suspense	acknowledge	conquer
condense	postpone	conqueror
immense	envelope	radiator
intense	liquid	mayor

dense   haughty   slaughter   curve   disease

peculiar	associate	scorch
familiar	association	horror
brilliant	appreciation	stubborn
Spaniard	official	Christian
Spanish	sufficient	positive

ancient   hymn   column   bruise   survive

courteous	rescue	skilful
courageous	virtue	pitiful
museum	issue	welfare
unusual	procession	fulfil
suggest	succession	ceremony

siege   salmon   Egypt   absurd   theatre